Find over 120 stickers at the back of this book!

My First Activity Book

ARCTURUS

This edition published in 2024 by Arcturus Publishing Limited
26/27 Bickels Yard, 151–153 Bermondsey Street,
London SE1 3HA

Authors: Lisa Regan and Harper Stewart
Illustrator: Kate Daubney
Editors: Violet Peto, Lucy Doncaster, and Lydia Halliday
Designers: Nathan Balsom and Lucy Doncaster
Managing Editor: Joe Harris
Design Manager: Jessica Holliland

ISBN: 978-1-3988-3663-1
CH011941NT
Supplier 29, Date 1123, PI 00005192

Printed in China

Pens and pencils at the ready—it's time to get puzzling! From mazes and number games to dot-to-dots and spot the difference puzzles, this book is packed with more than 130 activities and puzzles for you to enjoy. To make it even more fun, there are over 120 stickers! Complete the scenes for the first 10 puzzles with special stickers just for those pages, then get creative with the rest and use them to decorate whichever pages you like. What are you waiting for? Let's go!

Sunday Outing

What a lovely summer's day! Connect the dots to reveal
the rest of this hovering insect.

Ripe for the Picking

Ravi Racoon is gathering pears, and Geraldine Giraffe is gathering peaches.
Who gets to gather the most fruit?

Fun in the Sun

Oh, we do like to be beside the seaside!
Find each of the items that are shown on the side.

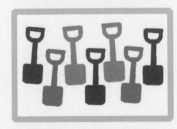

7

Flying High

Up, up, and away! Which of the tiles isn't part of the main picture?

A

B

C

D

E

9

Busy Bee

Connect the dots to give the bees a home!
Can you guess what Tara Tiger is collecting?

Puppy Parade

Which of the dogs is the same as the one in the photograph?

Strawberry Patch

It's a lovely day in the strawberry patch. How many strawberries can you find in this scene?

The Great Outdoors

Gracie Goat is very busy! Find each of the items that are shown on the side.

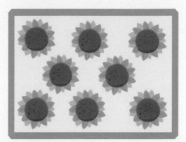

Enchanted Kingdom

Can you find all of the items shown in the panel on the right in this scene?

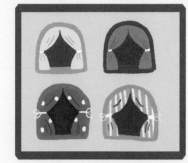
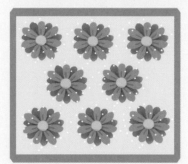

Party Piece

Felicity Fox is nearly ready for her party guests to arrive. What is the one thing she still needs to find? Connect the dots to see what it is!

Garden Delights

Can you find the names of three flowers hidden in these letters?
Cross out all of the other letters.

BHROSENXFTVIOLETLPNDAISYHQU

Something Missing

Yikes! These vehicles each have a wheel missing!
Look carefully to see which wheel
should go back on each vehicle.

A Walk in the Park

Tansy Turtle loves to walk in the sunshine. Guide her from the green gate to the blue gate, so she can enjoy all the sights.

START

FINISH

Listen to the Band

What a beautiful sound they make!
Which of the tiles isn't part of the main picture?

A

B

C

D

23

Toothy Teaser

Which of these clever crocodiles has the most teeth?
Look how clean and shiny their teeth are!

Mrs. Hop's Flowers

What a beautiful display! Draw more petals,
so that each flower has 10 petals.

Pretty as a Picture

Which of the pretty peacocks is a tiny bit different from the others?

Say Cheese!

Study this school photo, and then turn the page
to see which students have swapped places.

Say Cheese!

Can you remember who was sitting where? Then see who has swapped places.

Puppy Training

Which of the puppies walks nicely and makes it all the way to the cones at the end?

On the Seashore

Which of Sophie Bunny's seashells needs to go in each space to finish each pattern?

Matchmaking

Find each pair of fish, and use pens or crayons to
make the black-and-white ones match their partners.

Tasty Treats

Which of Rumiko Rabbit's delicious ice cream sundaes isn't quite the same as the others?

Look Outside

What has landed outside Stephanie's window?
Connect the dots to find out!

Lots of Lemurs!

Which of the silhouette shapes matches the lemur in the middle?

ID Parade

These guys are having a great time! See if you can find all these penguins in the picture:

A penguin on skates

A penguin with a red beak

A penguin wearing green glasses

Hocus Pocus

Welcome to Magical Merlin's school for wizards!
See if you can find all of the spellbinding items from the list.

Tiger Twins

Which two tigers are the same?

Hiding in the Jungle

The names of three jungle birds are hidden in these letters.
Can you find them? Cross out all of the other letters.

GRPARROTHBTOUCANWREAGLEKH

Time for a Change

Match each caterpillar to the butterfly it will turn into. Use the patterns to help you.

Feeling Good

Mrs. Hop is feeling happy today!
Can you find the word HAPPY
hidden just once in the grid?

```
H P A P P P Y H
H P A Y P A P Y
P A H P A H Y Y
Y A P P Y H A P
P H Y A P P H A
H A H A P P Y P
A P P Y H A P Y
P A H Y P P Y H
```

Magpie Treasures

Find a way through the jewels following them in this order.
You can move across and down, but not diagonally.

START

FINISH

Eggs-actly!

How many ostrich eggs can you count?
Are there the same number of eggs as there are ostriches?

In the Jungle

Study the jungle scene, then decide whether each of the sentences below is true or false.

The toucan is sitting on a branch.

The frog is red with black spots.

The blue butterfly is bigger than the yellow one.

There is a snake on the highest branch.

There are no orange flowers.

Jump for Joy

Which three pieces are needed to finish the puzzle?

A

B

C

D

E

Who's Who?

Write the correct name beneath each of the pictures.

- The horse is named Harry.
- Hugo has long, floppy ears.
- Hermione is black and white.

- Hector is a prickly character.
- The owl is named Huong.
- Himani is wearing a hat.

Going Underground

Help Pico Pig through the cave
to find the magnificent waterfall.

START

FINISH

I Can Count

Which are there more of, big black-and-white fish
or small black-and-white fish? Count them to find out!

Dressing Up

Finish the costumes by adding a hat and accessories,
then use your crayons to liven things up.

Toy Trucks

Which of Ricky Raccoon's trucks is a tiny bit different from the others?

Time for a Trim

Troy the hairdresser is ready for his next client! The names of three items he uses are hidden in these letters. Can you find them? Cross out all of the other letters.

Picnic in the Park

Kayla Koala has brought sandwiches to the picnic, and Bobby Badger has brought donuts. Who brought the most treats?

Catch of the Day

Which of the friends has managed to catch a fish?
Follow the lines to find out.

Beautiful Beads

Which of the scattered beads needs to go in each space to finish the pattern on the necklace?

You Try!

Use the grid lines to help you copy the picture into the blank space.

Market Day

It's very busy in the market today.
Can you spot six differences between the two pictures?

Party Animals

It's party time! Check out who's here,
then turn the page to see who has swapped partners.

Party Animals

Can you remember who was dancing together and see
who has swapped partners?

A Whale of a Time!

Can you find the word WHALE
hidden in the grid three times?

W A L E H L E A
H E W H A L E W
E W E A W H A H
A H L W H E A A
L A E H H W H L
E L W E A L H L
W E H L W H A E
W H A L E L H E

Traffic Jam

Find a way through the cars following them in this order.
You can move across and down, but not diagonally.

START

FINISH

My Marbles!

Tansy is collecting green marbles. Tony is collecting yellow marbles. Who can collect the most?

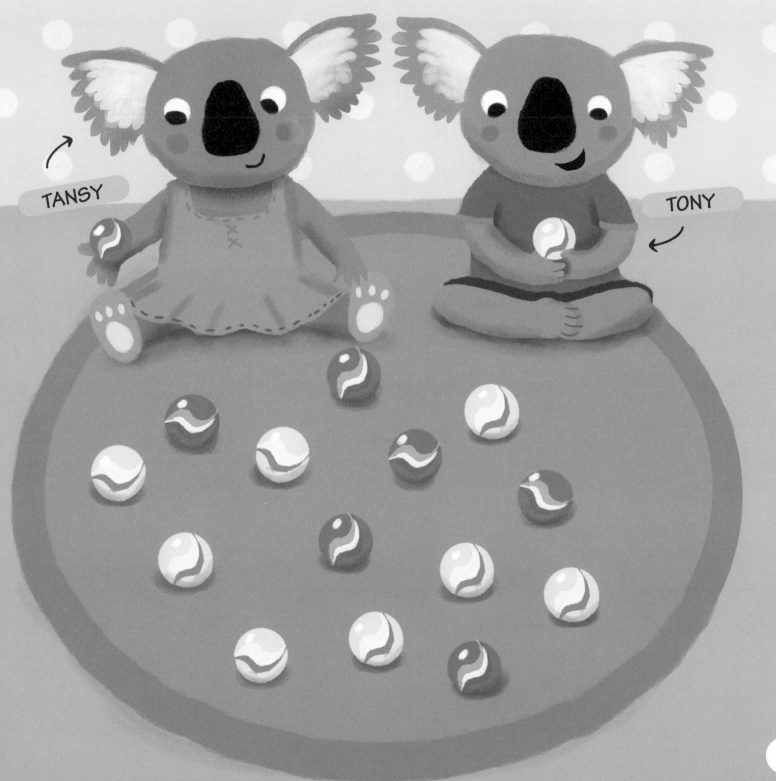

A Shady Character

Which of the silhouette shapes matches the sly fox in the middle?

Apples and Pears

Charlie Bear loves apples. Missy Bear loves pears.
Who gets the most of the fruit they like best?

Turtley Different

All of these turtles are different, apart from a pair of twins.
Can you spot the two that look the same?

64

From Me to You

What present does Charlie Bear have for Missy Bear?
Connect the dots to find out!

Heading for Home

Each bug lives in a house that coordinates with its hat and boots.
Which bug doesn't live on this street?

As Fast as a Fox

Fernando Fox is in a hurry! Help him drive from the forest to the stores before they close for the night.

START

FINISH

Taking Stock

Magical Merlin has made lots of potions! Help him count them,
and write the numbers on his stock list at the bottom.

A Lovely Lunch

What would you have for lunch if you could choose anything? Draw it here!

A Big Day Out

Study the beach scene, then decide whether each of the sentences below is true or false.

The surfers are all standing up.

The gull is eating a sandwich.

None of the crabs are red.

The pink shell is bigger than the others.

The blue-and-white beach ball is in the water.

Baking Buddies

Which three pieces are needed to finish the puzzle?

Not That Knit

Stephanie Stork has knitted scarves for all her friends.
Which one of them is a tiny bit different?

Fan Fun

Study this crowd, then turn the page
to see which fans have swapped places.

Fan Fun

Can you remember who was sitting where and see
who has swapped places?

Trash Raiders

Follow the wiggly lines to see who has made such a mess!

Planning Ahead

Rumiko Rabbit uses the same ingredients to make her world-famous pasta sauce. Which of the sets of ingredients is wrong?

Mix or Match?

Use the top picture and copy it with your pens and crayons—
or if you prefer, do your own thing and make it completely different!

Happy Times

Look at the two scenes below. Which two animals have left the picnic in the second scene? Which two have joined the friends?

Big Cat Quest

The names of three big cats are hidden in these letters.
Can you find them? Cross out all of the other letters.

A L I O N R Y T I G E R M E L E O P A R D P

I See Seahorses

Can you find a blue seahorse with green markings swimming among the seaweed?

In the Trees

Can you find all the tree-dwelling animals written in the grid?
BAT, FROG, LEMUR, OWL, PARROT, ROBIN, SLOTH, SNAKE

F R R A L S G T
S N A K E L A L
F P A R R O T E
R L S B H T W M
O E B H T H I U
B T A W O W L R
I N T O I U K O
N D S F R O G B

81

Ahoy There!

Look carefully at Bruno's pirate map.
Which of the small squares isn't actually from the map?

Ready, Set, Go!

Look carefully at these two pictures, and try to find six differences between them.

84

Time for Cake!

Kayla Koala is making a cake for Mrs. Hop's birthday! Help her finish the pattern of decorations on each tier by filling in the spaces.

Shell Spot

Luna Lemur is collecting seashells at the beach.
Can you spot the only seashell that does
not have an identical match?

Park Puzzle

Finn is lost in the park!
Can you help him find his way out?

START

FINISH

Crazy About Books

How many red books can you find in this library scene?

Bike Buddies

The bike race is complete! Trace each route from the top to the bottom of the map, then match the flags to each competitor to decide who took the shortest route.

Talent Show

This talented trio have won first prize!
Can you spot seven differences between these two pictures?

Roll Up! Roll Up!

Look at those acrobats go! Can you find all the items from the panel on the right in this scene?

Find the Fish

All of these fish are different, apart from a pair of twins. Can you spot the two that look the same?

Turtley Confused

Tony Turtle lives on the log in the middle of the lake, but he can't seem to remember the way home! Can you help him choose the correct route to get there?

Family Photo

Which three pieces are needed to complete the jigsaw puzzle of the Bear family portrait?

A

B

C

D

E

Eye of Newt

Help Merlin complete his magical mixture by following the potion order shown. You may move up, down, left, and right, but not diagonally.

START

FINISH

Beautiful Birds

Find the pairs of these pretty birds, and use pens or crayons to make the black-and-white one match its partner.

Spring Cleaning

Mrs. Hop needs your help to organize her beach shed.
Can you complete the pattern on each shelf by filling in the missing
items in the gaps?

Cloud Cover

Which three pieces are needed to finish this jigsaw puzzle?

A

B

C

D

E

Lunchtime!

Which of the construction workers is having a sandwich for lunch today? Follow the trails to find out!

Ahoy!

Match each pirate to their ship. Use the ships' sails to help you.

Kites

These kites look lovely up in the sky—but the last one needs finishing!
Follow the sequence, and decorate the blank kite using your pens and pencils.

Counting with Canoes

Which of the three canoes has the most passengers?

Party Time!

It's Mrs. Hop's birthday party!
Study the scene, then decide whether each
of the sentences below is true or false.

- Kayla Koala and Herman Hippo are holding the banner.
- Everyone is wearing a party hat.
- Bruno Bear is wearing red shoes.
- Mabel Mouse is dancing.
- There are seven slices of cake.

Happy Birthday, Mrs. Hop!

Busy Bus

The bus is crowded today! Can you find all the items
from the panel on the right in this scene?

Sparkle and Shine

Each of these necklaces has a twin. Can you spot the one necklace that does not have an identical match?

Eat Up!

What a tasty meal Rasheed Rooster has prepared! Study this photo, then turn the page to see which of the items have swapped places.

Eat Up!

Can you figure out which of the items have swapped places?

Shoe Shenanigans

Patrick Porcupine has lost his other shoe!
Can you help him find it?

Creating Cupcakes

What delicious treats! Find each pair of cupcakes, and use pens or crayons to make the black-and-white one match its partner.

Mighty Mountain

Which three pieces are needed
to complete the jigsaw puzzle?

A

B

C

D

E

Marsh Maze

This duck is looking for his mother.
Can you help him find her?

START

FINISH

Inching Along

Help this hungry caterpillar munch his way through the forest by following the leaf pattern. You may move up, down, left, and right, but not diagonally.

Watch Them Twirl!

Which of the tiles isn't part of the main picture?

A

B

C

D

Perfect Pizza

Which silhouette matches the picture of Masato Macaque?

Band Practice

Practice makes perfect! Study this picture of the orchestra,
then turn the page to see who has swapped places.

Band Practice

Can you figure out who has swapped places?

Pretty in Pink

Fernanda loves to show off her bright pink feathers! Can you find the word PINK hidden just once in the grid?

P	N	I	I	N	K	I	P
I	I	N	K	P	N	I	K	P
K	P	N	P	I	N	P	I
N	I	P	K	P	N	P	N
N	P	K	I	K	P	I	N
P	I	K	N	P	I	N	K
K	N	N	I	I	K	P	P
K	I	I	P	P	N	K	I

High Fliers

See if you can find all of these beautiful balloons:

- A balloon being piloted by a penguin
- A pair of matching balloons
- A red, white, and yellow balloon

Butterflies

Find each pair of matching butterflies, and use pens or crayons to make each black-and-white one match its partner.

Gone Fishing

Owen Owl loves to fish! Can you help him get to the perfect fishing spot?

START

FINISH

Travel Bug

Look at all the cool places Kayla Koala has visited! Study the framed photos, then decide whether each of the sentences below is true or false.

- Kayla has never been to a city.
- The cottage she visited was white and blue.
- Kayla has never seen snow.
- Kayla is in all of the pictures.
- In one of the pictures, Kayla is wearing a pink dress.

Jungle Jigsaw

Which three pieces are needed to complete this jigsaw puzzle?

A

B

C

D

E

Breakfast Time

All of these loaves of bread look identical,
apart from one. Can you spot it?

Splish–Splash!

Which of the tiles isn't part of the main picture?

A

B

C

D

129

High and Dry

Sunita is hanging up her washing.
Can you help her complete the pattern?
Which remaining clothes should she hang up
and where should they go?

Time for Lunch

The names of three types of food are hidden in these letters. Can you find them? Cross out all of the other letters.

JHKSANDWICHKJHSALADLHLIUPASTAHD

Movie Night!

Can you spot six differences between
these two scenes?

Dinnertime!

Paolo Panda is enjoying a plate of pasta! Can you find the silhouette that matches the main picture?

Brush, Brush, Brush!

Jerome Jaguar wants you to remember to take care of your teeth! Can you find the word BRUSH hidden just once in the grid?

S	H	R	U	B	R	U	B
R	U	S	H	S	H	B	R
U	R	R	B	U	H	S	R
S	H	U	R	B	H	S	U
B	R	B	R	U	S	H	R
U	S	H	R	U	B	S	H
B	U	S	H	B	U	R	S
S	H	U	R	B	R	H	B

It's a Jungle Out There!

Study this jungle scene, then turn the
page to see which of the animals have moved.

It's a Jungle Out There!

Can you figure out which animals have moved?

It's a Mouthful

Which pelican has caught the most fish?

Hats Off!

All of these hats are different, apart from a matching pair.
Can you spot the two that look the same?

Creative Creations!

Pablo Pigasso's students are amazing artists!
Can you complete the pattern of artworks on each line?

Tennis Team

Write the names above or below each team member using the clues.

- Geraldine is wearing a bandana.
- Fatima has the biggest ears.
- The goat is named Gallia.
- Peter has spots.
- Bobby is black and white.
- Sunita is next to Bobby and Fatima.

Hustle and Bustle

Can you find all these items
in the busy train station?

- A red suitcase
- A cat napping
- An elephant wearing a hat

Bowled Over

Can you help Missy find her lucky bowling ball?

- It is patterned.
- It contains yellow but not green.

It's Chilly Out Here!

Can you match these penguins to their eggs?

Get Creative!

Brighten up this image using your pens and pencils!

Stargazers

Look at the beautiful night sky! Can you spot six differences between these two pictures?

Who's There?

All of these sneaky spies are different,
apart from two in the same disguise.
Can you spot the matching pair?

High Up

Which climber will reach the top using the shortest route?

Off Your Rocker

One of these rocking horses is a tiny bit different. Which one is it?

Howdy There!

Study this picture, then turn the page to answer some questions about the scene.

Howdy There!

What can you remember without looking back?

- Was Panda's horse black or brown?

- How many snakes were there?

- Were the flowers on the cacti yellow or purple?

Ball Pit

How many of each ball can you spot in the ball pit?

Ice Sculpture

Who has won the ice sculpture competition? Follow the clues to find out! The winner is wearing the items listed in the yellow box.

- A hat
- Black boots
- A patterned scarf

Flower Power

Find a pair to each pretty vase, then use your pens and pencils to make the black-and-white one match its partner.

Soaring Through the Sky

Connect the dots to reveal this beautiful hovering bird.
Use your pens and crayons to add bright shades.

154

Shell Seekers

What pretty shells! Study the shoreline below, then decide whether each of the sentences is true or false.

- All the shells are unique.
- There are four pink shells.
- The blue shell is bigger than the green shell.
- There is a hermit crab inside the yellow shell.
- There are eight shells in total.

Answers

Page 4

Page 5

There are 7 pears and 9 peaches, so Geraldine Giraffe gets to gather the most fruit.

Pages 6–7

Pages 8–9

Page 10

Tara Tiger is collecting honey from a bees' nest!

Page 11

Pages 12–13

There are eight strawberries.

Pages 14–15

Pages 16–17

Page 18

Felicity Fox needs a party hat.

Page 19

Page 20

Page 21

Pages 22–23

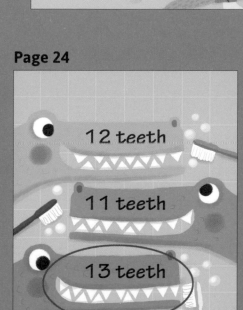

Page 24

12 teeth

11 teeth

13 teeth

Page 25

Page 26

Pages 27–28

These students have swapped places: Hippo and Bear; Tiger and Lemur.

Page 29

Page 30

Page 31

Page 32

Page 33

A spaceship has landed.

Page 34

Page 35

- A penguin on skates
- A penguin with a red beak
- A penguin wearing green glasses

Pages 36–37

Page 38

Page 39

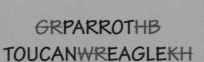

G̶R̶PARROT̶H̶B̶ TOUCAN̶W̶R̶EAGLE̶K̶H̶

Page 40

Page 41

Page 42

Page 43

No, there are not the same number of eggs and ostriches. There are four eggs, and there are five ostriches.

Page 44

- The toucan is sitting on a branch. TRUE
- The frog is red with black spots. FALSE—The frog is yellow with black spots.
- The blue butterfly is bigger than the yellow one. FALSE—The yellow butterfly is bigger than the blue one.
- There is a snake on the highest branch. TRUE
- There are no orange flowers. TRUE

Page 45

Page 46

HUONG
HERMIONE
HIMANI
HUGO
HECTOR
HARRY

Page 47

Page 48

There are five big black-and-white fish, and there are six small black-and-white fish. Therefore, there are more small black-and-white fish than there are big black-and-white fish.

Page 50

Page 51

~~OO~~SCISSORS~~TG~~BRUSH~~LI~~SHAMPOO~~V~~

Page 52

Kayla Koala brought seven sandwiches, and Bobby Badger brought six donuts, so Kayla Koala brought the most treats.

Page 53

Page 54

Page 56

Pages 57–58

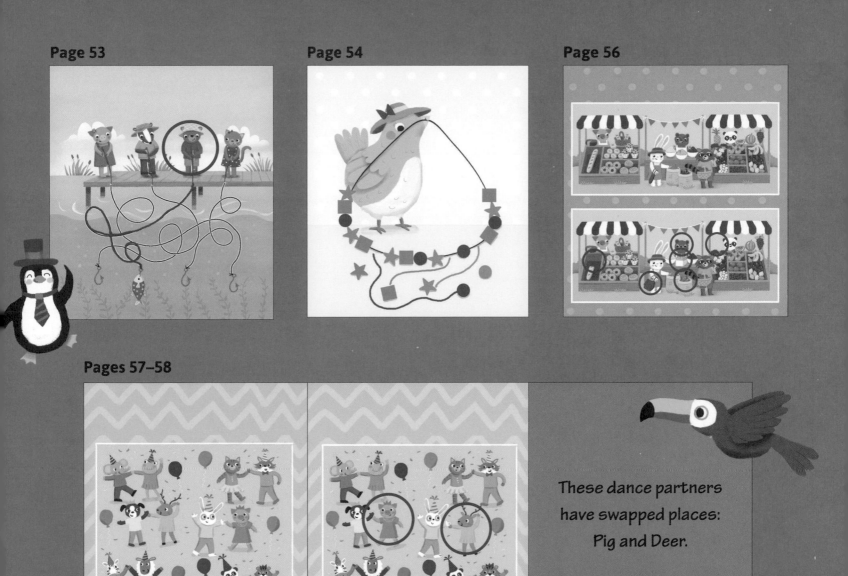

These dance partners
have swapped places:
Pig and Deer.

Page 59

```
W A L E H L E A
W H E W H A L E W
E A W E A W H A H
A H L W H E A A L
L A E H H W W H L
E L E W E A L H L
W E H L W H A E E
W H A L E L H E
```

Page 60

Page 61

Tansy can collect seven
green marbles, and Tony
can collect nine yellow
marbles, so Tony can
collect the most.

Page 62

Page 63

There are six pears and four apples, so Missy Bear gets most of the fruit she likes.

Page 64

Page 65

The answer is a hat.

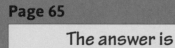

Page 66

Page 67

Page 68

Page 70

- The surfers are all standing up. FALSE— One surfer is lying down.
- The gull is eating a sandwich. FALSE— The gull is eating a fish.
- None of the crabs is red. TRUE

- The pink shell is bigger than the others. FALSE— The pink shell is smaller than the others.
- The blue-and-white beach ball is in the water. FALSE—It is on a towel.

Page 71

Page 72

Pages 73–74

These sports fans have
swapped places:
Frog and Lemur;
Cat and Dog.

Page 75

Page 76

Page 78

Panda and Frog have left the picnic—Horse and Squirrel have joined.

Page 79

ALIONRYTIGERMELEOPARDP

Page 80

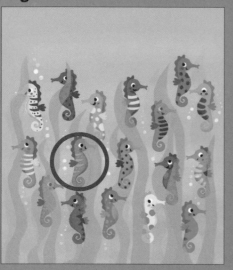

Page 81

```
F R R A L S G T
S N A K E L A L
F P A R R O T E
R L S B H T W M
O E B H T H I U
B T A W O W L R
I N T O I U K O
N D S F R O G B
```

Pages 82–83

Page 84

Page 85

Page 86

Page 87

Pages 88–89

There are six red books.

Page 90

The pig took the shortest route to the finish line.

Page 91

Pages 92–93

Page 94

Page 95

Page 96

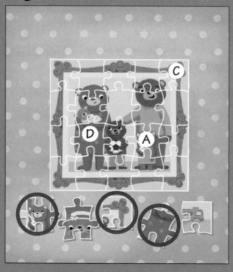

Page 97

Page 98

Page 99

Page 100

Page 101

Page 102

Page 103

Page 104

Page 105

- Kayla Koala and Herman Hippo are holding the banner. TRUE

- Everyone is wearing a party hat. FALSE—The fox is not wearing a party hat.

- Bruno Bear is wearing red shoes. FALSE— Bruno Bear is wearing blue shoes.

- Mabel Mouse is dancing. TRUE

- There are seven slices of cake. FALSE—There are nine slices of cake.

Pages 106–107

Page 108

Pages 109–110

These items have swapped places: The salad and the cup.

Page 111

Page 112

Page 113

Page 114

Page 115

Pages 116–117

Page 118

Pages 119–120

These orchestra members have swapped places: Panda and Cat; Crocodile and Flamingo.

Page 121

Page 122

- A balloon being piloted by a penguin

- A pair of matching balloons

- A red, white, and yellow balloon

Page 123

Page 124

Page 125

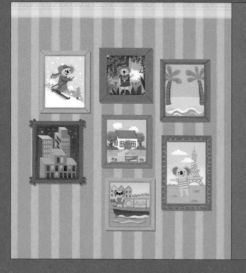

- Kayla has never been to a city. FALSE

- The cottage she visited was white and blue. TRUE

- Kayla has never seen snow. FALSE

- Kayla is in all of the pictures. FALSE

- In one of the pictures, Kayla is wearing a pink dress. TRUE

Page 126

Page 127

Pages 128–129

Page 130

Page 131

Page 132

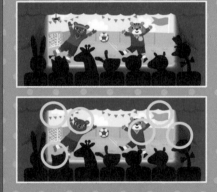

Page 133

Page 134

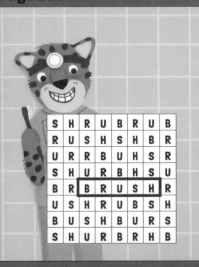

Pages 135–136

These animals have swapped places: The toucan and the frog; the purple bird and the butterfly.

Page 137

10 fish

11 fish

Page 138

Page 139

Page 140

BOBBY | SUNITA | FATIMA

GERALDINE | GALLIA | PETER

Page 141

- A red suitcase
- A cat napping
- An elephant wearing a hat

Page 142

Page 143

Page 145

Page 146

Page 147

The racoon used the shortest route to the finish.

Page 148

Page 150

Panda's horse was brown.

There were two snakes.

The flowers on the cacti were purple.

Page 151

5   3   7   8

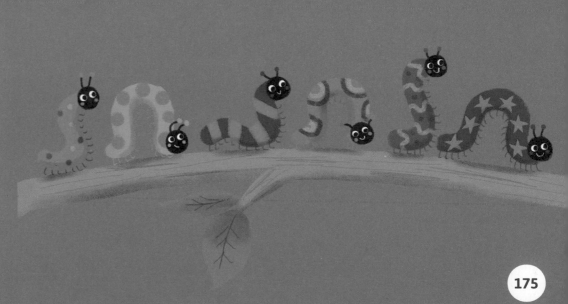

Page 152

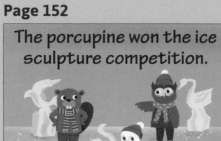

The porcupine won the ice sculpture competition.

Page 153

Page 154

Page 155

- All the shells are unique. TRUE

- There are four pink shells. TRUE

- The blue shell is bigger than the green shell. TRUE

- There is a hermit crab inside the yellow shell. FALSE—There is a hermit crab inside the purple shell.

- There are eight shells in total. TRUE